To:
- - - - - - - - - - - - - - - - - - - -
. . . - - - - - - - - - - - - - - - - - -

Message:
- - - - - - - - - - - - - - - - - - - -
- - - - - - - - - - - - - - - - - - - -
- - - - - - - - - - - - - - - - - - - -
- - - - - - - - - - - - - - - - - - - -

From:
- - - - - - - - - - - - - - - - - - - -

The Heart of a Teacher

© 2003 Christian Art Gifts, RSA
 Christian Art Gifts Inc., IL, USA

Text © Karla Dornacher

First edition © 2018 Christian Art Publishers
PO Box 1599, Vereeniging, 1930, RSA

Designed by Christian Art Publishers

Images used under license from Shutterstock.com

Printed in China

ISBN 978-1-4321-2713-8

19 20 21 22 23 24 25 26 27 28 – 14 13 12 11 10 9 8 7 6 5

The Heart
OF A

TEACHER

CHRISTIAN ART PUBLISHERS

Your *love*
has given me great joy
and encouragement.
Philemon 7

I wanted to swing so high in the sky,
the other kids could, I wanted to try.
I sat down alone and held on tight,
I kicked my feet with all my might.
But the swing stayed still, it didn't sway
and I learned a special lesson that day.

Sometimes we need a push to start,
a gentle nudge from a caring heart.
You saw in me the potential to soar
you encouraged me to try so much more!

Whenever I struggled, kicking my feet,
you never let me give up in defeat.
So thank you, Teacher, for giving me
the push I needed to be all I could be.

THANK YOU,

Teacher...

for *loving* me
unconditionally ...

for helping me
RUN THE RACE
of life without
giving up ...

for making me
feel like a winner
when I do my best
and don't give in ...

for teaching me
truth with wisdom

and understanding ...

for preparing me to walk with
confidence and courage into
a world of endless opportunities.

I AM *fearfully* & wonderfully **MADE.**

Psalm 139:14

God created me
to be one of a kind.
There's no one else like me!
I can do some things really good.
But some things,
no matter how hard I try,
I will never be good at.
That's just the way God made me.
I'm glad you don't expect me
to be someone I'm not,
but you always encourage me
to be the best me I can be.

Thank you!

From the *fruit* of their lips people are filled with good things, and the work of their **hands** brings them *reward.*

Proverbs 12:14

Put your *hope*
in the LORD.
Travel steadily
along His path.

Psalm 37:34

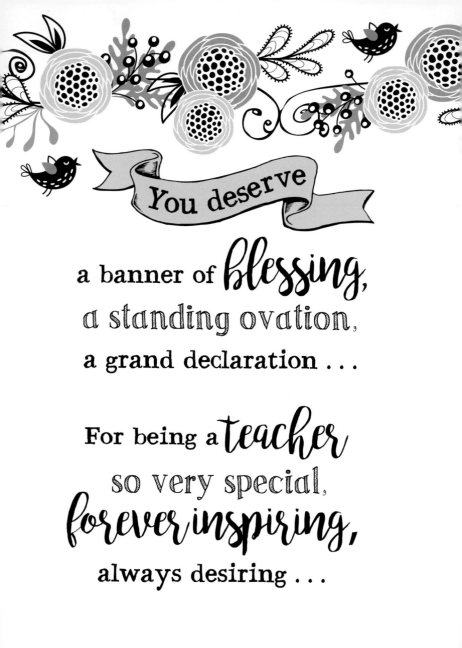

You deserve

a banner of *blessing,*
a standing ovation,
a grand declaration . . .

For being a *teacher*
so very special,
forever inspiring,
always desiring . . .

To instill within the *heart*
of each child,
a *love* for learning,
an eternal yearning...

To *grow* in **wisdom,**
and gain understanding,
a true education,
a new generation . . .

the labor of your heart!

Blessed

are those who find
wisdom, those who
gain understanding,
for she is more
profitable than silver
and yields better
returns than gold.

Proverbs
3:13-14

FOR
HE SHALL GIVE
His
angels
charge over you,
to keep you
in all your
ways.

Psalm 91:11

It is no accident
you're my teacher.
God knew you were
the perfect one.
He gave you the passion
to mold and shape me,
to challenge my mind
and make it fun.

I know at times
you must grow weary,
with all the work
you have to do;
so I pray for God
to give you rest
so you don't give up ...
because I need you!

Great
are the works
of the Lord;
they are pondered
by all who
delight in them.

Psalm 111:2

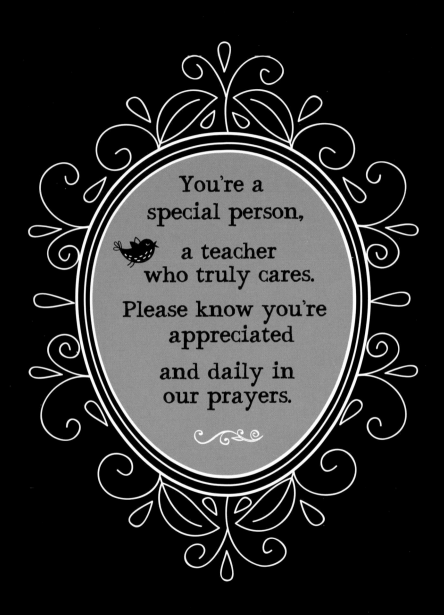

You're a
special person,

a teacher
who truly cares.

Please know you're
appreciated

and daily in
our prayers.

Dear Jesus,

Bless this teacher
with the light of Your love,
a heavenly vision – a gift from above.

Give her eyes to see, Lord, what no one else can,
that spark of the future she holds in her hand.

May she catch a glimpse of lives yet untold,
bright hope for tomorrow in each child to unfold.

May she shine like a star, reflecting Your glory,
as she is a chapter in each child's lifelong story.

Amen.

You shine like stars in the universe
as you hold out the word of life.

Philippians 2:15-16

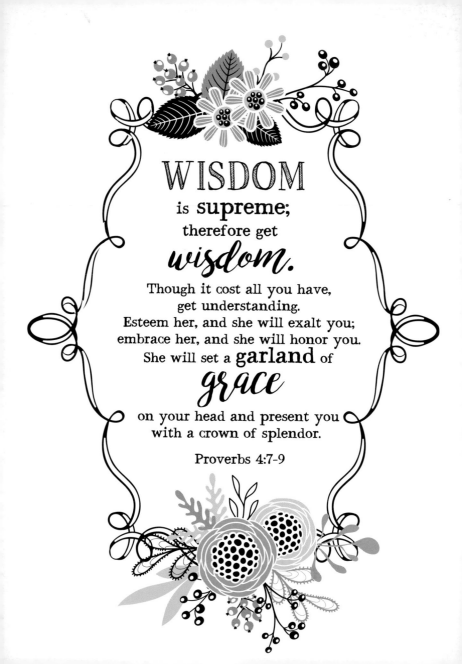

WISDOM

is **supreme**;
therefore get

wisdom.

Though it cost all you have,
get understanding.
Esteem her, and she will exalt you;
embrace her, and she will honor you.
She will set a **garland** of

grace

on your head and present you
with a crown of splendor.

Proverbs 4:7-9

The fear of the
LORD
is the beginning of
knowledge
& the *hope*
of the
next generation.

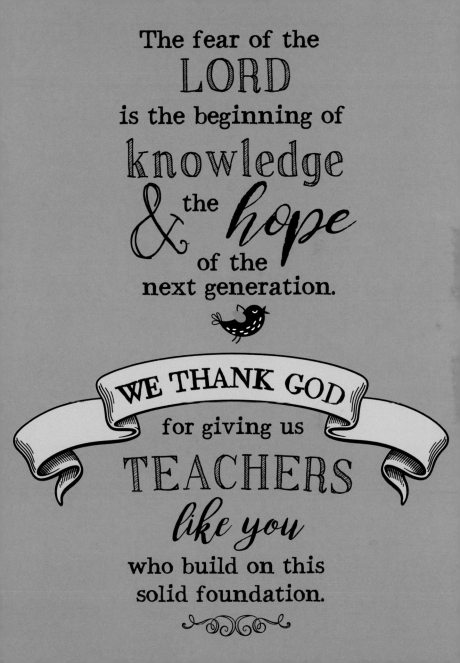

WE THANK GOD
for giving us
TEACHERS
like you
who build on this
solid foundation.

Dear Jesus,

Thank You for this teacher
and all the love and energy
she pours into each child
You've placed in her care.

I ask You, Lord,
to replenish her strength this day.
Pour out, into her life,
a drink of refreshing and blessing
that will fill her cup
and overflow her heart!

Amen.

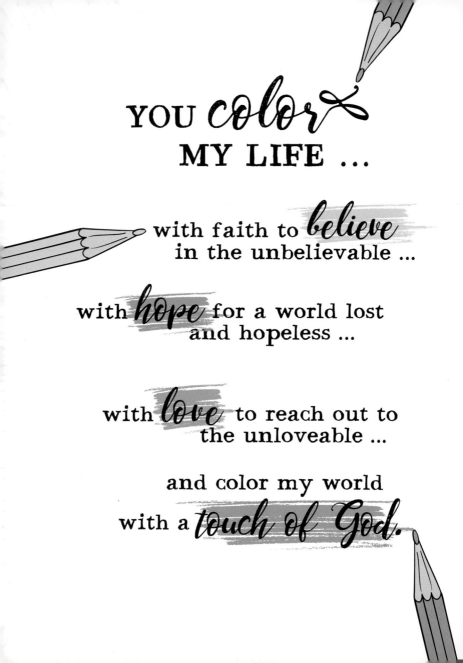

YOU *color*
MY LIFE ...

with faith to *believe*
in the unbelievable ...

with *hope* for a world lost
and hopeless ...

with *love* to reach out to
the unloveable ...

and color my world

with a *touch of God.*

You
MAKE A
difference!

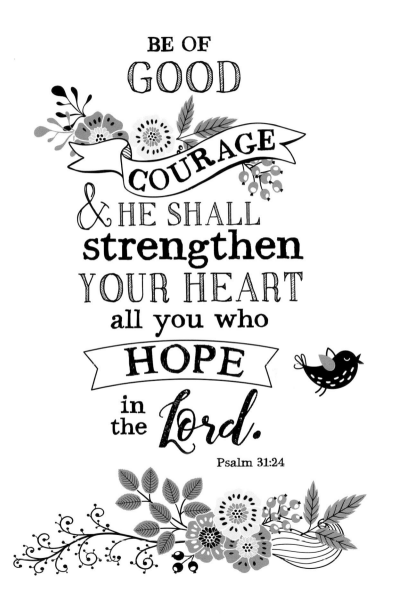

BE OF
GOOD
COURAGE
& HE SHALL
strengthen
YOUR HEART
all you who
HOPE
in
the Lord.

Psalm 31:24

A is for Apples
AND
Angels

they're both sweet
and so are you!

B is for Birds
AND
Blessings

singing the praises
of all you do!

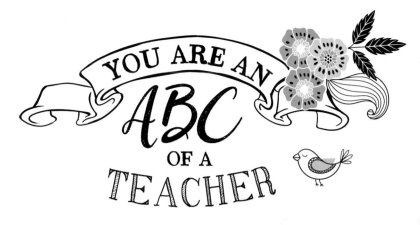

YOU *Accept*
each one of us for who we are
with our individual weaknesses, strengths,
and unique God-given personalities.

YOU *Bless*
us with your passion and enthusiasm
to share the wonders of the universe in ways
that stir our desire for more.

YOU *Challenge*
our hearts to pursue the love of learning,
our minds to explore the world around us,
and our spirits to seek truth above all else.

May the *Lord bless* you and protect you.
May the *Lord* smile on you
and be *gracious* to you.

May the *Lord* show you His favor
and give you His *peace.*

Numbers 6:24-26

I applied my heart
to what I observed and
learned a lesson
from what I saw.

PROVERBS
24:32

Thank you,
Teacher ...

for you've been a great example
as I've watched you day by day.
You don't just teach me by the book,
it's more than what you say ...
it's how your heart communicates
through your actions and your caring,
that helps me apply to my life
the knowledge that you're sharing.

Wisdom

She is a tree of life to those who embrace her; those who lay hold of her will be blessed ...

PROVERBS 3:18

The
righteous eat
to their
hearts' content.

PROVERBS 13:25

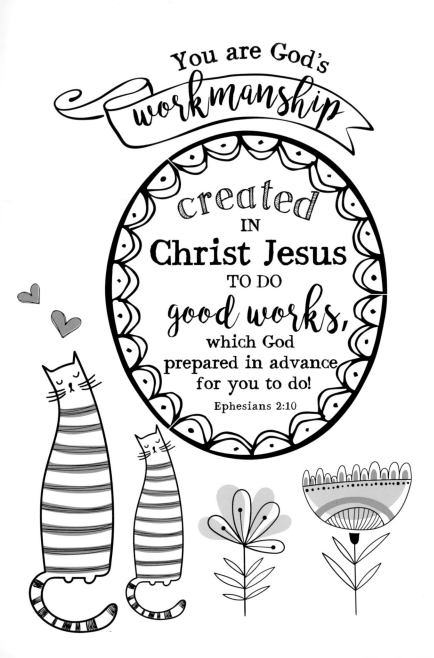

We thank God
for you and the good work
you do teaching minds,
touching hearts,
and taking the
time to care!

Our children enter
your classroom
with countless questions
to be asked,
seeking honest answers
and wise counsel,
knocking on the doors of
their futures yet unknown.

We are thankful that God
has entrusted you
with the knowledge to
answer the questions,
the wisdom to guide
and direct, and the key to
open the door to the next
step of their journey.

"Give, and
you will receive.
Your gift will return to you
in full – pressed down,
shaken together to make room
for more, running over,
and poured into your lap.
The amount you give will
determine the amount
you get back."

Luke 6:38

Reading, 'riting and 'rithmetic
are the basics of good education.
They are the skills our minds will use
to live a life of exploration.

For the future is filled with treasures
far greater than silver and gold –
a wealth of knowledge to discover –
the riches of wisdom untold.

So thank you, Teacher, for all you do,
for laying a solid foundation,
for paving the path to all my tomorrows
with hope in the next generation!

NOW *faith* IS THE SUBSTANCE OF THINGS *hoped* FOR, THE EVIDENCE OF THINGS NOT SEEN.

HEBREWS 11:1

Dear Teacher,

You don't know me ... not really.
You don't know my **inner thoughts**
or secret fears.

You don't know how much I struggle
to be liked and accepted.
You don't know how much I want
someone to see me and **believe** in me.

But
when you
smile at me
and say
" you can do it,
I know you can",
I feel special ...
and I think you know more than
I think you know.

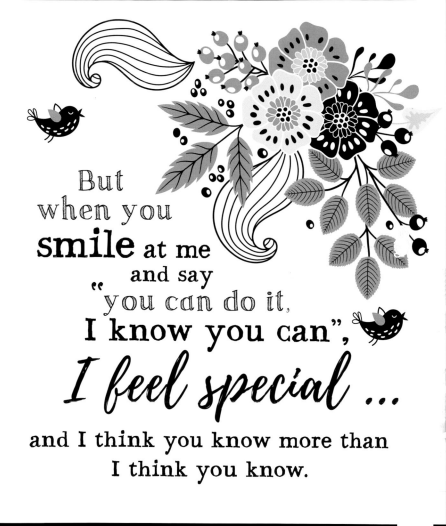

I HAVE
not stopped
giving
thanks
for you,
remembering you
in my prayers.

Ephesians 1:16